# Choosing a School For Your Child

Office of Innovation and Improvement
**United States Department of Education**

**U.S. Department of Education**
Margaret Spellings
*Secretary*

**Office of Innovation and Improvement**
Morgan S. Brown
*Assistant Deputy Secretary*

Original production of this book was led by Jack Klenk, director, Office of Non-Public Education, Office of Innovation and Improvement, and Cynthia Hearn Dorfman, former director of Communications, Office of Innovation and Improvement; and funded by the Office of Parental Options and Information in the Office of Innovation and Improvement, John Fiegel, director, as part of the Parental Information and Resource Centers Program.

First published March 2005. Revised August 2007.

To obtain copies of this report in English or Spanish,

write to: ED Pubs, Education Publications Center, U.S. Department of Education, P.O. Box 1398, Jessup, MD 20794-1398;

or fax your request to 301-470-1244;

or e-mail your request to: edpubs@inet.ed.gov;

or call in your request toll-free: 1-877-433-7827 (1-877-4-ED-PUBS). If 877 service is not yet available in your area, call 1-800-872-5327 (1-800-USA-LEARN). Those who use telecommunications device for the deaf (TDD) or a teletypewriter (TTY), should call 1-877-576-7734;

or order online at www.edpubs.org.

This book is also available on the Department's Web site at:
http://www.ed.gov/parents/schools/find/choose

On request, this publication is available in alternate formats, such as Braille, large print or computer diskette. For more information, please contact the Department's Alternate Format Center 202-260-0852 or 202-260-0818.

# Contents

# List of Parent Tips

Dear Parents,

Do you remember when your child was born, how your child quickly wrapped all five fingers around your one? Your child will continue to grasp your hand throughout childhood and youth. You are your child's first and lifelong teacher. And, as a parent and teacher, you will make important decisions for your child.

Some of the most important decisions you will make are about your child's education. You want your child's school to meet the same goals of high academic achievement you have set. You may want your child's school to reflect the values of your family and community. In other words, you want to choose a school that is a good fit for your child. In an increasing number of communities in our nation, you now have the ability to do so.

This booklet, *Choosing a School for Your Child*, is a type of "decision tool" that can help you navigate the process of choosing a school. It explains some of the public school choices now available in many communities and covers private school options that may be available as well. It outlines steps that you can follow to help you make a thoughtful choice, and it includes questions that you might want to ask when going through the process.

In addition, this booklet highlights new options for your child's education provided in the federal law, the *No Child Left Behind Act*. The law allows parents whose children are in public schools that need improvement or are unsafe, to choose other public schools or take advantage of free tutoring or extra educational help.

The law also supports the growth of more independent public charter schools and funds some services for children in private schools. Finally, it mandates states and local school districts to provide a wealth of new information to help you make informed educational choices for your child.

School choice can help give every child an excellent education. It is amazing what can happen when parents get involved. School choice gives you more opportunities to achieve your expectations for your child. Armed with options and information, you can be a powerful advocate for your child.

I offer you *Choosing a School for Your Child* as a tool with practical information to help you make informed decisions about your child's education. I wish you success with this challenge.

Sincerely,
Margaret Spellings
Secretary
U.S. Department of Education

For additional resources on choosing a school, you can
visit the U.S. Department of Education's page for parents at
http://www.ed.gov/parents/landing.jhtml
or the page on school choice at
http://www.ed.gov/nclb/choice

# Choosing a School

Parents have a growing array of options in choosing a school, though the extent of the options varies from state to state. The enactment of the landmark *No Child Left Behind Act* of 2001; the rapid growth of the charter school movement; the increasing number of states enacting scholarship and tax credit programs for students to attend private schools; the expansion of privately funded scholarship programs for low-income children; and the growing acceptance of homeschooling have all increased the choices available to families.

Parents can exercise choice in many ways. The most common way may be in choosing where to live based on the public school district or neighborhood schools. In many areas, parents can choose from neighborhood schools, charter schools or other public schools of choice, or transfer their child to another public school (in or out of district). They can also select a private school (religious or secular) or teach their child at home.

*Choosing a School for Your Child* offers step-by-step advice on how to choose among the schools available to your child. It identifies important factors you may want to consider before making a decision. As you and your child visit different schools, you may want to consider the questions in each section of this booklet.

## Why Should You Choose Your Child's School?

No one cares more about your child's welfare than you do. No one else will be more careful to see that your child is well educated and well treated in school. You know your child's personality, strengths and weaknesses. You know the interests that light up your child's eyes. You know the values that your family wants a school to respect.

Choosing your child's school may also make you more confident that she will be taught effectively and treated fairly. Choosing your child's school carefully is an important way you can help your child achieve all that he can be. This is a head and a heart decision. Don't be afraid to heed your own informed and intuitive wisdom.

# Learn What Choices Are Available to You

Different schools offer alternatives in teaching styles, content, and learning opportunities. This section briefly describes some types of schools you may find.

## Public Schools

### Neighborhood Public Schools

Many parents choose to send their children to the public school in their neighborhood, according to an assignment system developed by the school district. Attending a neighborhood public school can make it easy for your child to get to school, to work with classmates on group projects, and to visit friends. These schools are often anchors in a community.

### Other Public Schools

You may want to investigate other public schools. In an increasing number of districts, you can choose to send your child to a specialized public school. These schools of choice often emphasize a particular subject or have a special philosophy of education. One school might emphasize science, art, or language study. Another might offer a firm code of conduct, a dress code, or a rigorous traditional academic program.

Another may be an alternative school designed to respond to students who are insufficiently challenged by the regular school program, who are likely to drop out, or who have behavioral or substance abuse problems. These schools, often small, work to make students feel they belong. Some states also offer second chance schools or clinics for students who have dropped out of regular schools and now want to complete their education.

- **Charter Schools**

  Charter schools are public schools of choice that operate with freedom from many of the local and state regulations that apply to traditional public schools. Charter schools allow parents, community leaders, educational entrepreneurs, and others the flexibility to innovate, create and provide students with increased educational options. Charter schools exercise increased autonomy in return for stronger accountability. They are sponsored by designated local, state, or other organizations that monitor their quality and integrity while holding them accountable for academic results and fiscal practices.

- **Magnet Schools**

  Magnet schools are designed to attract students from diverse social, economic, ethnic, and racial backgrounds by focusing on a specific subject, such as science, technology, or the arts. Some magnet schools require students to take an exam or demonstrate knowledge or skill in the specialty to qualify to go to the school, while others are open to students who express an interest in that area.

- **Virtual Schools**

  Instead of taking classes in a school building, students can receive their education using a computer through a virtual school. Virtual schools have an organized curriculum. Depending on the state and district, students can take the full curriculum or individual classes. Some school districts have used these online schools to offer classes that will help students learn at their own pace. Virtual education is sometimes used in remote areas for specialized or advanced courses that are not available in the immediate area. This type of studying is also called "distance learning."

- **Advanced Placement and International Baccalaureate Programs**

  Advanced Placement (AP) courses offer rigorous content, and at the end of a course students can take the national Advanced Placement exam. If they score well on the exam, many colleges and universities will grant college credit for completing the course. The International Baccalaureate (IB) is a program of rigorous academic courses. Students who graduate from the program receive an

International Baccalaureate diploma that is recognized by colleges and universities throughout the world. Other students may choose not to take the full IB curriculum but pursue certificates in individual areas. Elementary and middle schools may also offer components of the IB program.

# Nonpublic Schools

In addition to public schools, there may be a variety of religious and other nonpublic schools available in your area or boarding schools away from home. These schools of choice have been part of the fabric of American education since colonial days. These schools have been established to meet the demand to support parents' differing beliefs about how their children should be educated.

## Religious Private Schools

The majority of nonpublic schools are religious. Many are affiliated with a denomination, local church, or religious faith such as Roman Catholic, Protestant, Greek Orthodox, Jewish, Muslim, Buddhist, or other.

## Secular Private Schools

There are also many nonpublic schools without a religious identity or affiliation. Some of these private schools are preparatory schools designed to prepare students for college. These schools often have a traditional or elite reputation and a long history. Other schools are based on a particular educational philosophy or approach to learning, such as Montessori or Waldorf schools; have a special education focus, such as schools for the deaf or blind; or have been established for families and children who may be dissatisfied with various aspects of conventional schools.

## Home Schools

Homeschooling is an option for a growing number of parents. Some parents prepare their own materials and design their own programs of study, while others use materials produced by companies specializing in homeschool materials. Some take advantage of virtual school programs or other educational resources available on the Internet. Of course, exercising this option may require major changes in how your family lives. Teaching your children at home is an ambitious undertaking, requiring time, planning, creativity, and commitment. Be sure to check with your state because different states have different requirements for homeschooling.

# Selecting a School for Your Child

How do you pick the best school for your child? Whether you are choosing a public or private school or homeschooling, whether or not you are paying tuition, careful planning is a must. The following sections have questions for you to consider, with workspace for you to write down your thoughts, as you go through the process of choosing a school for your child. Remember, you are looking for a school that will make the educational experience for your child and you as rewarding as possible.

## Write Down Five Things That Are Most Important to You

You may wish to write down five things that are most important to you as you consider the choice of a school. As you go through the selection process, you may want to add to and revise your list.

1. ............................................................

............................................................

2. ............................................................

............................................................

3. ............................................................

............................................................

4. ............................................................

............................................................

5. ............................................................

............................................................

## Four Steps for Selecting the School That Is Right for Your Child

# Step 1

Consider your child & your family.

Start your search for the best school by thinking about what you want a school to do for your child. Perhaps your child has special language or education needs. Keep these in mind. After all, you know your son or daughter better than anyone else does.

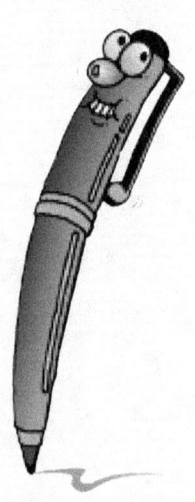

## Your Child's Needs

Does your child need a more structured environment?

Does your child need a less structured environment?

Does your child need more challenging work?

Does your child need more individual attention?

Does your child generally need extra help or more time to complete an assignment?

Does your child have any special learning needs?

Does your child need an environment that fosters creativity?

Does your child need an English language acquisition program?

## Your Child's Learning Style

Does your child learn best by seeing how things work?

Does your child learn best by reading about how something works?

Does your child learn best by listening?

Does your child like to participate in discussions?

Does your child like to learn through physical activity?

Is your child logical or mathematical?

Is your child musical or artistic?

Does your child like to learn in groups?

Does your child like to work alone?

Read the questions and jot down some notes to help you with your decisions.

## Location of School

Do you want your child to go to a school within walking distance of your home?

Can your child's talents be nurtured outside your neighborhood?

How far are you willing to have your child bused?

How far are you willing to drive your child to school?

Does your child want to be in a school with his or her friends?

Do you want your child to go to a school near your after-school care? Near where you work? Near a close relative?

Does your child have any special transportation needs that must be considered in choosing a school?

Read the questions and jot down some notes to help you with your decisions.

# Parent Tip:

**Know Your Options Under the No Child Left Behind Act for Children in Public Schools That Are "In Need of Improvement"**

*Parents of children in public schools designated as "in need of improvement" can choose another public school or supplemental educational services (free tutoring).*

If your child's public school receives federal Title I funds, it must let you know how well the students in the school are learning. The school district must contact you if the school does not meet the academic standards set by the state for two consecutive years. You can find out how well your school is doing by looking at the school's report card.

If your child's school has been identified by the state as in need of improvement, the school district must give you the choice of keeping your child in that school or sending him or her to another public school.

If your child attends a school that has needed improvement for more than a year, your school district is required to give you a list of organizations and institutions that provide tutoring or extra help outside of the regular school day. This extra help is called "supplemental educational services." If your child is eligible for this help, and your income is low, the school district may pay for these extra services. Such services may include before- and after-school tutoring in reading, other language arts, or math.

If you have not heard from your public school about whether the school is "in need of improvement" and whether your child qualifies to receive supplemental educational services, contact the school or the school district and ask for the person(s) in charge of choice and supplemental services programs. You can also go to your state department of education's Web site for a list of schools in need of improvement and approved supplemental educational services providers. If you have difficulty finding these lists, call the U.S. Department of Education at 1-888-814-6252 for help in reaching your state contact, or go to the U.S. Department of Education's Web site at http://www.ed.gov/about/contacts/state/index.html for a list of contacts in your state.

# Four Steps for Selecting the School That Is Right for Your Child

# Step 2

## Gather Information About Schools

If you were looking to buy a car, vacuum cleaner, or refrigerator, you could talk to friends and family and find information on the Internet, in consumer magazines, or in other published resources. Similarly, when investigating schools, you may also have to make phone calls, collect written material from different schools and look for reports in your local paper to get the information you need. You can check public school report cards (see Parent Tip) and go to parent fairs and school open houses.

You can find reliable school information online on sites such as www.greatschools.net and www.schoolmatters.org, as well as other sites listed in the Resources section of this booklet. The hard work will be worth your while if you find a school that brings out the best in your child.

Along with the schools' curricula and philosophy, you will want to know about school policies and services. Parents may also wish to consider the after-school programs a school offers, for example, sports, clubs, tutoring, or academic enrichment. Some schools have after-school activities funded by the U.S. Department of Education's 21st Century Community Learning Centers program. These centers provide educational activities outside of the regular school hours—before and after school or during summer vacation—that complement what is taught in school. You may also want to ask if the school has supplemental educational services, including free tutoring, that are offered outside of the regular school hours under *No Child Left Behind*.

Read the questions and jot down some notes to help you with your decisions.

## Curriculum

Does the school have a strong program of core academic subjects such as English, history, mathematics, science, arts, and foreign languages?

What courses does the school offer in addition to the core subjects?

What evidence is there that the school is effectively teaching students to read?

Does the school have a special focus or theme for the curriculum?

Does the school offer challenging courses such as Advanced Placement, International Baccalaureate, and high school honors courses?

Does the school provide enrichment opportunities for all students? For gifted students?

Does the school have extracurricular activities that support what is taught?

Is there an effective English language acquisition program for children who need it?

If your child has special learning needs, does the school have a curriculum and the necessary supports to appropriately accommodate those needs?

## Approach to Learning

Does the school have a particular approach to teaching and learning (e.g., group projects, individual performance, frequent testing)?

If yes, do you think your child will enjoy and learn from this approach?

Does the school do all it can to make sure each child learns? Does it provide opportunities for children to get extra help when they need it?

Is the school staff able to communicate in the language that your child understands?

Are children with limited English language skills, learning disabilities, or other special needs learning and performing well on tests?

What is the homework policy? Does it match your expectations for how much homework your child should do?

Do you want your child to go to a single-sex (all-boy or all-girl) school, or a coeducational school?

How large are the classes?

Read the questions and jot down some notes to help you with your decisions.

## Academic Performance

How do the school's test scores compare to those of other schools? (Check the school's report card if it is a public school or ask for information from the school if it is a private school. See **"Parent Tip"** on school report cards.)

In the past few years, have test scores risen or declined? How does the school explain the rise or decline?

How well have children similar to yours performed on these tests?

How do students moving on to the next level of schooling perform in their new schools?

How many students leave the school before completing the last grade?

What special achievements or recognition has the school received?

## Behavior Policy

What does the school do to help develop character and citizenship?

What is the discipline policy? How does the school handle students who misbehave?

Are teachers fair in their responses to students? Does the school have a program and supports to prevent and address behavior problems?

Are students allowed to leave school by themselves?

What measures has the school taken to ensure safety? What security measures are in place?

# Parent Tip:

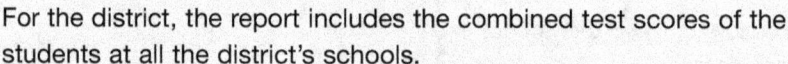

## Check the School District's Report Card for Public Schools

*No Child Left Behind* requires school districts that receive federal funds to provide a report card on how its schools and the school district are doing. For individual schools, the report card includes whether the school has been identified for school improvement and how its students performed on state tests compared to other students in the school district and the state.

For the district, the report includes the combined test scores of the students at all the district's schools.

## Public school report cards should include:

Students' scores on state tests, broken out by student subgroups;

How many students performed at the "basic," "proficient," and "advanced" levels on the tests;

Graduation rates;

Numbers and names of schools that need to improve in the district;

Qualifications of teachers; and

Percentage of students who were not tested.

## Behavior Policy (continued)

What is the policy on school absences? How does the school encourage daily attendance?

Do school personnel call parents when students are absent?

Does the school have a drug and alcohol abuse prevention program?

Does the school have a dress code? Do students wear uniforms?

## Safety

Is the school safe?

How does the school prevent and handle problems with drugs, alcohol, and tobacco?

How does the school prevent and handle violence, bullying, harassment, and other forms of abusive behavior?

What measures does the school take to ensure safety? What security measures are in place?

What is the school's relationship with the local police?

Is there a police officer on duty during school hours and for extracurricular activities?

What information is available on serious crime in the school?

What information is available on students bringing weapons to school?

Does the school have an emergency plan for local and national emergencies?

What does the school do to ensure that parents and all school administrators know the emergency plan?

Are there drills?

How does the school notify parents about emergency closings? How does the school communicate with parents in other languages?

## Special Offerings

What extracurricular activities does the school offer after school or on weekends?

Do all students have the opportunity to participate in extracurricular activities?

What interscholastic activities are available to students?

What intramural activities are available to students?

What activities receive the most attention and resources?

Are there school and student publications?

Does the school sponsor field trips? Are they available to all students?

Are publications for parents available in other languages?

## Facilities and Services

Is there a well-stocked library where students can check out books and do research? Are reading materials available in other languages? Is there interlibrary loan?

Is time provided in the day for students to go to the library?

Do students have access to computers and to the Internet in the classroom and library?

Is use of the Internet monitored?

Read the questions and jot down some notes to help you with your decisions.

Is there an auditorium or a large room for school assemblies?

Is a school nurse on duty daily?

Is there a cafeteria, and does the school offer a nutritionally well-balanced lunch program? Breakfast program?

Is supervised before- and after-school care offered?

Are there tutoring programs?

Are counseling services available to students?

Is the school accessible to children with mobility limitations?

## Admissions Procedures for Public Schools of Choice and Private Schools

Is there an application process?

What is the application deadline?

Is anything else required in the application (test scores, interview, recommendations, application fees, etc.)?

Are test scores required for admission? What are the ranges of scores for admitted students?

Do admissions requirements include a portfolio, an audition or statement of interest?

Are there any other admissions requirements?

Are admissions requirements published in languages other than English?

## Additional Questions About Private Schools

What is the tuition?

Is there a payment plan?

Is there a sliding scale for tuition, based on parish, church affiliation, or family income?

What are the other fees and expenses (room and board, uniforms, books, transportation, lab and computer fees, activity fees)?

What scholarships and loans are available?

Are students or their parents required to be of a particular faith?

Does the school have a policy on student participation in religious instruction and worship?

Does the school close for religious and federal holidays?

Does the school have the same schedule as the local public school?

## Additional Questions About Home Schools

Have you identified curriculum materials for your child, and how much they will cost?

Is there a suitable place for your child's study and instruction?

Do you, your spouse, or another homeschooling parent have adequate free time to be available to your homeschooling child?

Read the questions and jot down some notes to help you with your decisions.

Do other families in your area home-school their children?

Is there a support group of home-schoolers near you?

If you are interested in some outside instructional support, have you checked your local library, parks department, scouting organizations, public and private schools, and similar resources?

Have you searched the Web for resources on instruction, legal issues, support groups, and other matters?

Have you identified other resources you will need?

Have you checked state regulations? (They are usually available on the web or from your local public school or school district.)

# Parent Tip:

## Know Your Options Under the No Child Left Behind Act for Children in Public Schools That Are Unsafe

*Parents of children in unsafe public schools may have the opportunity to transfer their children to safe public schools.*

Children should not have to attend unsafe schools. *NCLB* requires public schools to offer parents the opportunity to transfer their children to safe public schools if the state designates their public elementary or secondary schools as unsafe. Your children must also be offered opportunities to transfer to other public schools in the district if they have been the victims of violent crimes while in school or on school grounds. To find out if your child's school has been designated as unsafe by the state, you can contact either your local school district office or the state department of education. A list of state contacts can be found at http://www.ed.gov/about/contacts/state/index.html.

## Four Steps for Selecting the School That Is Right for Your Child

# Step 3

### Visit & Observe Schools

Contact the schools you are interested in and make an appointment for a visit. If possible, tour the schools during regular school hours and visit a few classes. Avoid visiting schools during the first or last week of a semester in order to get a realistic sense of how the school operates.

A good way to have your questions answered is to schedule an appointment with the school principal. If possible, attend an open house, parent-teacher meeting, or other school function that would also provide valuable information about the attitudes of staff, students, and parents.

Listen closely to what teachers say about the school. The teachers will be the adults closest to your child, and you will want to know if they are well prepared, dedicated, and happy in their work.

## Culture

Is the school secretary helpful and friendly?

Is the school orderly and neat?

What do the bulletin boards look like?

How is student work displayed?

How does the school communicate with students and parents (weekly/monthly newsletter, e-mail, Web site)?

Do the students appear to be courteous, happy, and disciplined?

Is there a welcoming attitude toward all parents?

How are the students with diverse learning needs (e.g., students with disabilities and students with limited English proficiency) treated?

Do the teachers appear to be helpful and friendly?

## Principal

What is the principal's philosophy about education?

What is the principal's attitude toward discipline?

In what extracurricular activities is the principal most interested?

What is the principal's reputation in the community?

Is the principal usually at the school and available to talk to parents?

Does the principal get to know the students?

Read the questions and jot down some notes to help you with your decisions.

How often does the principal observe teachers?

What does the school do to keep good teachers and improve teacher performance?

How does the principal respond to parental concerns/complaints?

What is the principal's attitude toward students with diverse learning needs (e.g., students with disabilities and students with limited English proficiency)?

According to the principal, what are the school's strengths?

According to the principal, what are the school's weaknesses?

According to the principal, where can the school improve?

## Teachers

How do teachers grade student work?

Do teachers have high expectations for all students to achieve to high academic standards?

How do teachers inform students of their expectations?

Do teachers share the course content and objectives with parents?

When and how frequently are teachers available for parent conferences?

Do teachers assign homework? Is it rigorous? Frequent? Sufficient?

Are the teachers highly qualified to teach in their subject areas (do they know the subjects they are teaching)?

Read the questions and jot down some notes to help you with your decisions.

Do teachers have the skills and knowledge to address students with special learning needs?

Are specialized staffs available to address the special learning needs of a child (e.g., speech therapist, psychologist or aides)?

Do the teachers know the individual students in their classes?

Are teachers willing to provide extra help to students?

What is the school's policy regarding teacher response to parent inquiries?

Do teachers have Web sites with class notes and other information for students and parents?

## Students

What is the attendance rate for students?

What do students say about the principal?

What do students say about the teachers?

Do the students have school spirit?

What do students say about homework?

Do students participate in and enjoy field trips?

Do students feel safe and secure at the school?

What do student publications say?

What else do students say about the school?

## Parent and Community Involvement

How does the school encourage parental involvement?

What are the ways parents can get involved?

Are parents encouraged to volunteer?

Does the school have an active parent-teacher organization?

Does the school hold meetings and events at times when parents can attend?

How well attended are back-to-school nights by parents?

Are families expected to be involved with homework?

How frequently does the school communicate with parents?

Are community leaders involved with the school?

Does the school partner with local businesses and organizations?

Are parents involved in the development of school policies?

## Reputation

How is the school regarded in the community?

How is the school viewed by other parents?

Is the school respected by other schools, particularly those that receive its students (when they move to the next level)?

Read the questions and jot down some notes to help you with your decisions.

Has the school won any awards?

Do people move to the community to go to the school?

What do the graduates of the school say?

Have graduates from the school made significant contributions to the community and their field of choice?

# Parent Tip:

## 10 Things to Look for in a School

High expectations

Busy students

Great teachers

Great principal

Vibrant parent-teacher organization

Children are neither invisible nor scared to be at school

Gut reaction that this is the school for your child

Rigorous curriculum

Families like yours are welcome, and their concerns are acknowledged

You are satisfied with the school's results on standardized tests and school report cards

*Source: Minnesota Department of Education, Office of Choice and Innovation*

## Four Steps for Selecting the School That Is Right for Your Child

# Step 4

**Apply to the School(s) You Choose**

Once you select the school(s) that you think will be best for your child, you will go through a process of applying to a school (or schools) of your choice and enrolling your child. Consider applying to more than one school, in case your child is not admitted to their first choice.

You will want to begin this process as early as possible in order to ensure you meet all the deadlines.

Admissions processes can vary. Your child may need to be tested or interviewed, and you may need to provide a school transcript, recommendations, or other information. It would be helpful to learn about admissions criteria for the schools. You will want to double check to be sure you have accurate information on when and how to apply.

## Select one or more schools to apply to

To which schools do you want to apply?

What is the application deadline at each school?

## Submit paperwork and applications before the deadlines

Have you completely filled out the application for each school?

Have you included all of the required additional information with the application (deposit, student transcript, test scores, letters of recommendation)?

Have you submitted applications before the deadline set by each school?

## Follow up

Have you contacted each school to check on your child's application status?

When will the schools notify you that your child has been admitted?

When will you need to notify the school that your child plans to attend?

When will you notify the schools that your child will not attend?

Read the questions and jot down some notes to help you with your decisions.

# Parent Tip:

## Start Early & Cover All the Steps

Begin the process of choosing
a school as early as possible.

Find out as soon as possible about the
deadlines for applying to the schools you
are considering.

Note that some schools require applications
much earlier than others.

### Keep These 4 Steps in Mind:

Step 1. Consider your child and your family.

Step 2. Gather information about schools.

Step 3. Visit and observe schools.

Step 4. Apply to the school(s) you choose.

# Congratulations

Congratulations on all the planning you have done to reach this point. Your child will benefit tremendously from your active concern and involvement with his or her education. By collecting information, talking to other parents, visiting schools, and exercising your right to choose, you can now take the lead in making sure your son or daughter gets the best possible education. However, this is only the beginning. By staying involved in your child's education, encouraging your child to work hard, and providing additional opportunities to learn at home and in the community, you can help your child go further still. Remember it is your right, as well as your responsibility, to seek the very best education for your son or daughter.

# Parent Tip:

Find Helpful Resources at the
U.S. Department of Education's
Choice Web Site

**www.ed.gov/nclb/choice**

The U.S. Department of Education's Office of Innovation and Improvement (OII) provides information regarding the choices available to parents seeking the best educational opportunities for their children.

Office of Innovation and Improvement
U.S. Department of Education
400 Maryland Ave. S.W.
Washington, DC 20202

www.ed.gov/about/offices/list/oii

202-205-4500

# Resources

## Web Sites for Directories & Other Information

*Choice Web Site* www.ed.gov/nclb/choice

Many other Web sites provide information related to school choice.

*Information for parents from the U.S. Department of Education* at www.ed.gov (Click on the "Parents" box.)

*Council of Chief State School Officers* (links to state education agencies where you can learn about school performance and supplemental educational services providers) at www.ccsso.org

*GreatSchools.net* (school profiles and comparative performance data) at www.greatschools.net

*National Center for Education Statistics, U.S. Department of Education* (search for public and private schools) at http://nces.ed.gov/globallocator

*Office of Non-Public Education, U.S. Department of Education* (links to nonpublic school organizations, private school locator, and other information about nonpublic education) at www.ed.gov/about/offices/list/oii/nonpublic/index.html

*Parental Information and Resource Centers* (directory of centers across the country) at www.ed.gov/programs/pirc/grantees.html

*SchoolMatters.org* (comparative performance data) at www.schoolmatters.org

*U.S. Charter Schools* (information about charter schools) at www.uscharterschools.org

*Web sites for homeschoolers:* The Web has many resources, including instructional materials, assistance on legal issues, links to support groups, and others. Web sites for homeschoolers are too numerous to list here, but a search on terms such as "homeschool" or "homeschooling" should lead you to those sites that best match your interests and needs.

# Parent Information Organizations

There are many organizations that can provide valuable information to assist parents seeking to choose a school. The following are a few examples:

**Alliance for School Choice**
1660 L Street, NW
Suite 1000
Washington, DC 20036
202-280-1990
www.allianceforschoolchoice.org

**Black Alliance for Educational Options (BAEO)**
1710 Rhode Island Avenue, NW
Suite 1200
Washington, DC 20036
202-429-2236
www.baeo.org

**Center for Education Reform (CER)**
1001 Connecticut Avenue, NW
Suite 204
Washington, DC 20036
202-822-9000
www.edreform.com

**Council for American Private Education (CAPE)**
13017 Wisteria Drive #457
Germantown, MD 20874
301-916-8460
www.capenet.org

**Hispanic Council for Reform and Educational Options (Hispanic CREO)**
2600 Virginia Avenue, NW
Suite 408
Washington, DC 20037
1-877-888-2736
www.hcreo.org

*Note:* **The lists on the Resources pages provide examples that may be useful for parents. No endorsement by the U.S. Department of Education of these Web sites, books, or organizations should be implied.**

# Acknowledgments

This publication was adapted from *Choosing a School for Your Child* by Susan Perkins Weston, with contributions from Joe Nathan and Mary Anne Raywid, originally published in 1989 by the Office of Educational Research and Improvement, U.S. Department of Education. The original edition was prepared in 2005 by the Office of Innovation and Improvement.

We are grateful for the reviewers from outside the U.S. Department of Education who commented on the original version of this book.

# Your Contacts

Name. . . . . . . . . . . . . . . . . . . . . . . . . . . . . . . . . . . . . . . . . . . . . . . . . . . . . . . . . . . .

Organization . . . . . . . . . . . . . . . . . . . . . . . . . . . . . . . . . . . . . . . . . . . . . . . . . . . . . . .

Address. . . . . . . . . . . . . . . . . . . . . . . . . . . . . . . . . . . . . . . . . . . . . . . . . . . . . . . . . . . .

Phone . . . . . . . . . . . . . . . . . . . . . . . Fax . . . . . . . . . . . . . . . . . . . . . . . . . . . . . . . .

E-mail . . . . . . . . . . . . . . . . . . . . . . . Web site. . . . . . . . . . . . . . . . . . . . . . . . .

Name. . . . . . . . . . . . . . . . . . . . . . . . . . . . . . . . . . . . . . . . . . . . . . . . . . . . . . . . . . . .

Organization . . . . . . . . . . . . . . . . . . . . . . . . . . . . . . . . . . . . . . . . . . . . . . . . . . . . . . .

Address. . . . . . . . . . . . . . . . . . . . . . . . . . . . . . . . . . . . . . . . . . . . . . . . . . . . . . . . . . . .

Phone . . . . . . . . . . . . . . . . . . . . . . . Fax . . . . . . . . . . . . . . . . . . . . . . . . . . . . . . . .

E-mail . . . . . . . . . . . . . . . . . . . . . . . Web site. . . . . . . . . . . . . . . . . . . . . . . . .

Name. . . . . . . . . . . . . . . . . . . . . . . . . . . . . . . . . . . . . . . . . . . . . . . . . . . . . . . . . . . .

Organization . . . . . . . . . . . . . . . . . . . . . . . . . . . . . . . . . . . . . . . . . . . . . . . . . . . . . . .

Address. . . . . . . . . . . . . . . . . . . . . . . . . . . . . . . . . . . . . . . . . . . . . . . . . . . . . . . . . . . .

Phone . . . . . . . . . . . . . . . . . . . . . . . Fax . . . . . . . . . . . . . . . . . . . . . . . . . . . . . . . .

E-mail . . . . . . . . . . . . . . . . . . . . . . . Web site. . . . . . . . . . . . . . . . . . . . . . . . .

Name. . . . . . . . . . . . . . . . . . . . . . . . . . . . . . . . . . . . . . . . . . . . . . . . . . . . . . . . . . . .

Organization . . . . . . . . . . . . . . . . . . . . . . . . . . . . . . . . . . . . . . . . . . . . . . . . . . . . . . .

Address. . . . . . . . . . . . . . . . . . . . . . . . . . . . . . . . . . . . . . . . . . . . . . . . . . . . . . . . . . . .

Phone . . . . . . . . . . . . . . . . . . . . . . . Fax . . . . . . . . . . . . . . . . . . . . . . . . . . . . . . . .

E-mail . . . . . . . . . . . . . . . . . . . . . . . Web site. . . . . . . . . . . . . . . . . . . . . . . . .

Name. . . . . . . . . . . . . . . . . . . . . . . . . . . . . . . . . . . . . . . . . . . . . . . . . . . . . . . . . .

Organization . . . . . . . . . . . . . . . . . . . . . . . . . . . . . . . . . . . . . . . . . . . . . . . . . . . . . . .

Address. . . . . . . . . . . . . . . . . . . . . . . . . . . . . . . . . . . . . . . . . . . . . . . . . . . . . . . . . . .

Phone . . . . . . . . . . . . . . . . . . . . . . . . . . Fax. . . . . . . . . . . . . . . . . . . . . . . . . . . . . .

E-mail . . . . . . . . . . . . . . . . . . . . . . . . . . Web site. . . . . . . . . . . . . . . . . . . . . . . . . .

Name. . . . . . . . . . . . . . . . . . . . . . . . . . . . . . . . . . . . . . . . . . . . . . . . . . . . . . . . . .

Organization . . . . . . . . . . . . . . . . . . . . . . . . . . . . . . . . . . . . . . . . . . . . . . . . . . . . . . .

Address. . . . . . . . . . . . . . . . . . . . . . . . . . . . . . . . . . . . . . . . . . . . . . . . . . . . . . . . . . .

Phone . . . . . . . . . . . . . . . . . . . . . . . . . . Fax. . . . . . . . . . . . . . . . . . . . . . . . . . . . . .

E-mail . . . . . . . . . . . . . . . . . . . . . . . . . . Web site. . . . . . . . . . . . . . . . . . . . . . . . . .

Name. . . . . . . . . . . . . . . . . . . . . . . . . . . . . . . . . . . . . . . . . . . . . . . . . . . . . . . . . .

Organization . . . . . . . . . . . . . . . . . . . . . . . . . . . . . . . . . . . . . . . . . . . . . . . . . . . . . . .

Address. . . . . . . . . . . . . . . . . . . . . . . . . . . . . . . . . . . . . . . . . . . . . . . . . . . . . . . . . . .

Phone . . . . . . . . . . . . . . . . . . . . . . . . . . Fax. . . . . . . . . . . . . . . . . . . . . . . . . . . . . .

E-mail . . . . . . . . . . . . . . . . . . . . . . . . . . Web site. . . . . . . . . . . . . . . . . . . . . . . . . .

Name. . . . . . . . . . . . . . . . . . . . . . . . . . . . . . . . . . . . . . . . . . . . . . . . . . . . . . . . . .

Organization . . . . . . . . . . . . . . . . . . . . . . . . . . . . . . . . . . . . . . . . . . . . . . . . . . . . . . .

Address. . . . . . . . . . . . . . . . . . . . . . . . . . . . . . . . . . . . . . . . . . . . . . . . . . . . . . . . . . .

Phone . . . . . . . . . . . . . . . . . . . . . . . . . . Fax. . . . . . . . . . . . . . . . . . . . . . . . . . . . . .

E-mail . . . . . . . . . . . . . . . . . . . . . . . . . . Web site. . . . . . . . . . . . . . . . . . . . . . . . . .

# Your Contacts

Name. . . . . . . . . . . . . . . . . . . . . . . . . . . . . . . . . . . . . . . . . . . . . . . . . . . . . .

Organization . . . . . . . . . . . . . . . . . . . . . . . . . . . . . . . . . . . . . . . . . . . . . . . . .

Address. . . . . . . . . . . . . . . . . . . . . . . . . . . . . . . . . . . . . . . . . . . . . . . . . . . . .

Phone . . . . . . . . . . . . . . . . . . . . . . Fax . . . . . . . . . . . . . . . . . . . . . . . . . . . .

E-mail . . . . . . . . . . . . . . . . . . . . . . Web site. . . . . . . . . . . . . . . . . . . . . . .

Name. . . . . . . . . . . . . . . . . . . . . . . . . . . . . . . . . . . . . . . . . . . . . . . . . . . . . .

Organization . . . . . . . . . . . . . . . . . . . . . . . . . . . . . . . . . . . . . . . . . . . . . . . . .

Address. . . . . . . . . . . . . . . . . . . . . . . . . . . . . . . . . . . . . . . . . . . . . . . . . . . . .

Phone . . . . . . . . . . . . . . . . . . . . . . Fax . . . . . . . . . . . . . . . . . . . . . . . . . . . .

E-mail . . . . . . . . . . . . . . . . . . . . . . Web site. . . . . . . . . . . . . . . . . . . . . . .

Name. . . . . . . . . . . . . . . . . . . . . . . . . . . . . . . . . . . . . . . . . . . . . . . . . . . . . .

Organization . . . . . . . . . . . . . . . . . . . . . . . . . . . . . . . . . . . . . . . . . . . . . . . . .

Address. . . . . . . . . . . . . . . . . . . . . . . . . . . . . . . . . . . . . . . . . . . . . . . . . . . . .

Phone . . . . . . . . . . . . . . . . . . . . . . Fax . . . . . . . . . . . . . . . . . . . . . . . . . . . .

E-mail . . . . . . . . . . . . . . . . . . . . . . Web site. . . . . . . . . . . . . . . . . . . . . . .

Name. . . . . . . . . . . . . . . . . . . . . . . . . . . . . . . . . . . . . . . . . . . . . . . . . . . . . .

Organization . . . . . . . . . . . . . . . . . . . . . . . . . . . . . . . . . . . . . . . . . . . . . . . . .

Address. . . . . . . . . . . . . . . . . . . . . . . . . . . . . . . . . . . . . . . . . . . . . . . . . . . . .

Phone . . . . . . . . . . . . . . . . . . . . . . Fax . . . . . . . . . . . . . . . . . . . . . . . . . . . .

E-mail . . . . . . . . . . . . . . . . . . . . . . Web site. . . . . . . . . . . . . . . . . . . . . . .

Name. . . . . . . . . . . . . . . . . . . . . . . . . . . . . . . . . . . . . . . . . . . . . . . . . . . . . . . . . . . . . . .

Organization . . . . . . . . . . . . . . . . . . . . . . . . . . . . . . . . . . . . . . . . . . . . . . . . . . . . . . . . . .

Address. . . . . . . . . . . . . . . . . . . . . . . . . . . . . . . . . . . . . . . . . . . . . . . . . . . . . . . . . . . . . . .

Phone . . . . . . . . . . . . . . . . . . . . . . . . . Fax. . . . . . . . . . . . . . . . . . . . . . . . . . . . . . .

E-mail . . . . . . . . . . . . . . . . . . . . . . . . Web site. . . . . . . . . . . . . . . . . . . . . . . . .

Name. . . . . . . . . . . . . . . . . . . . . . . . . . . . . . . . . . . . . . . . . . . . . . . . . . . . . . . . . . . . . . .

Organization . . . . . . . . . . . . . . . . . . . . . . . . . . . . . . . . . . . . . . . . . . . . . . . . . . . . . . . . . .

Address. . . . . . . . . . . . . . . . . . . . . . . . . . . . . . . . . . . . . . . . . . . . . . . . . . . . . . . . . . . . . . .

Phone . . . . . . . . . . . . . . . . . . . . . . . . . Fax. . . . . . . . . . . . . . . . . . . . . . . . . . . . . . .

E-mail . . . . . . . . . . . . . . . . . . . . . . . . Web site. . . . . . . . . . . . . . . . . . . . . . . . .

Name. . . . . . . . . . . . . . . . . . . . . . . . . . . . . . . . . . . . . . . . . . . . . . . . . . . . . . . . . . . . . . .

Organization . . . . . . . . . . . . . . . . . . . . . . . . . . . . . . . . . . . . . . . . . . . . . . . . . . . . . . . . . .

Address. . . . . . . . . . . . . . . . . . . . . . . . . . . . . . . . . . . . . . . . . . . . . . . . . . . . . . . . . . . . . . .

Phone . . . . . . . . . . . . . . . . . . . . . . . . . Fax. . . . . . . . . . . . . . . . . . . . . . . . . . . . . . .

E-mail . . . . . . . . . . . . . . . . . . . . . . . . Web site. . . . . . . . . . . . . . . . . . . . . . . . .

Name. . . . . . . . . . . . . . . . . . . . . . . . . . . . . . . . . . . . . . . . . . . . . . . . . . . . . . . . . . . . . . .

Organization . . . . . . . . . . . . . . . . . . . . . . . . . . . . . . . . . . . . . . . . . . . . . . . . . . . . . . . . . .

Address. . . . . . . . . . . . . . . . . . . . . . . . . . . . . . . . . . . . . . . . . . . . . . . . . . . . . . . . . . . . . . .

Phone . . . . . . . . . . . . . . . . . . . . . . . . . Fax. . . . . . . . . . . . . . . . . . . . . . . . . . . . . . .

E-mail . . . . . . . . . . . . . . . . . . . . . . . . Web site. . . . . . . . . . . . . . . . . . . . . . . . .

# Notes

# Notes